THE SACRIFICE: When Transition Looks Like Chaos

The Sacrifice

When Transition Looks Like Chaos

YOUMIE JEAN FRANCOIS

Copyright © 2024 by Youmie Jean Francois

All rights reserved. No part of this book may be reproduced in any manner whatsoever without written permission except in the case of brief quotations embodied in critical articles and reviews.

Published by Youmie Jean Francois
Website: www.hernameisyoumie.com
Instagram: @hernameisyoumie

Second Edition: June 2024
Cover design by Kristina Liburd, Youmie Jean Francois
Interior design by Kristina Liburd, Youmie Jean Francois

Printed in the United States of America
Hardcover ISBN: 979-8-9914710-0-8

Contents

Foreword   xi

PART I: ENCOUNTERING CHAOS

The Sacrifice   3

Passover Trip   5

PART II: NAVIGATING PAIN AND LOSS

Invitation from grief   11

Dating Apps   13

Injured   15

Kryptonite   17

Unfiltered Anger   19

Avoidance   21

Preservation   23

Delusion or Hope?   25

PART III: SELF-DISCOVERY AND REFLECTION

Clarity	31
And then there were two	33
Closure	35
Your standards are too high	37
Wrong Location	39
Confidence Vampires	41
It's Personal	43
Real Talk	45
Careful	47
Just so you know	49
The sharpest knife	51
Silence	53
Playing Small	55
Advice	57
Your Strong friend	59
Fraudulent	61
Scenes from an immigrant's life	63
How disappointing	65

PART IV: GROWTH AND TRANSFORMATION

Inner child vs Inner Teens	71
Inner teen healing	73
You're Responsible	75
Hopelessness	77
Trauma Response	79
Triggers	81
You never got to meet her	83
To the strong black woman	85
What you can control	87
Patterns	89
To be clear	91
Genuine love	93
Scenes from an immigrant's life (part 2)	95
Speak	97
Leaving poverty	99
Mediocrity	101
Behind in life	103
Listen	105
Fake healed	107

Sit in it	109
Loneliness	111
Hard truth	113
How to wait	115
The thing is	117
Favoritism	119
Happiness	121
The truth about Faith	123
In the midst of it	125
Prayer is	127
Access Denied	129
Courage	131
Waiting on the right time.	133
Doubt	135
A powerful prayer	137
Prosperity	139
Prosperity (part 2)	141
The 7 C's of Success	143
He kept a tab.	145
Doing it alone	147

Contents ~ ix

Habitual	149
Blinded by Image	151
What I know for sure	153
Epilogue	157

Foreword

I've had these thoughts in my head for a number of years. Many of them are revelations that came through hardships. Heartbreak is a great teacher, poverty is a great motivator, healing is a powerful form of self-love, anger hardens your heart, and peace is a great indicator of being loved boldly. Transition often feels like chaos, If you happen to pick up this book my hope for you is simple. Surrender.

Part I: Encountering Chaos

The Sacrifice

Let your heart break,
I'll put it back together. -God

Passover Trip

If loving my blackness was so easy for you
Why was protecting it such a challenge for you?
Your people pleasing ways was quick to show compassion and a lending ear to those who didn't consider me "pure."
Oh how I wish you would have let rage consume you just once for my defense.
Unfortunately, I was left to guard my own heart and pride.
You're left with the possibility of feeling bad about it,
I'm left with the wound of your betrayal.

Meditation Pause

Take a deep breath in like you're
smelling your favorite flower,
now blow it out like you're blowing out a candle.

Part II: Navigating Pain and Loss

Invitation from grief

Ending things with you was an immediate invitation to grief.
I'm going to be here for a while aren't I?
I can't afford to rush this
I must experience every stage of it.
The same way I experienced you at the highest of high.
This low is torture, but the only way out is through right?
Okay.
Let's get started, then.

Dating Apps

You think I didn't have the same options available to me after we ended?

Like the apps weren't available for me to swipe?

Like I couldn't get under bodies to make up for the times that I felt sexually frustrated just to help me move on a bit faster?

You think I didn't meet someone new that I vibed with that made me feel good, someone all my friends felt were my equal?

Someone that I enjoyed having conversations with,

someone that fulfilled all the lust inside of me.

Someone that helped me forget about the years that I put into what I thought would be forever?

I had options.

They were swift, consistent, honest, fun, and available.

But I wasn't.

My spirit wouldn't allow my heart to take vengeance with my body.

My spirit wouldn't allow me to use and wound others because I refused to face the pain of us.

I chose the restless nights.

the tossing and turning,

the soaked pillow sheets,

the loneliness,

the anger,

the resentment,

the memories of what we built, and the acceptance of what we will never be again.
I don't blame you for choosing the route that you chose for your healing.
We were always different in the way that we dealt with pain.
I was quick to run away, and you were quick to find comfort with others.
I just want you to know that I had options, and I chose differently.
And you could have too...

Injured

My ego is too bruised to not let my rage be known.
So excuse me if I'm not careful with my words.

Kryptonite

Rejection is the egos kryptonite.

Unfiltered Anger

I hate that you got your healing faster than I did.
To see that you're happier apart from me.
I have every right to tell everyone all the ways you broke me,
made me insecure,
made my body sick,
made me financially stressed.
Wait.
Perhaps it's not that you got your healing faster than I did,
but that you got it without me.
Damn.

Avoidance

Pain
Avoid it.
Reject it.
Deny it.
Whatever you do,
Just don't feel it.

Preservation

How you left me broken was stronger than my love to fight for you.
Call it self-preservation.

Delusion or Hope?

It hurts my pride to tell you how I feel.
I know the longer we're apart the stronger you'll get.
The easier it will be for your mind to convince your body to replace me.
Your heart though, it won't be that easy.
It still belongs to me.

Meditation Pause

Take a deep breath in like you're
smelling your favorite flower,
now blow it out like you're blowing out a candle.

Part III: Self-Discovery and Reflection

Clarity

Years down the line,
You will have a moment of clarity.
There, you'll realize why I was so private.
Why your inconsistency assisted in my uncertainty about us.
Why I always felt uneasy about the way your family treated me.
Why your friends at that time weren't aligned with me.
Why I believed you didn't really need any of those things you pursued to be great in your career.
When you have that moment,
I will be married to the person that valued my privacy, my need for consistency, and when I share my discomfort about members of his family not being kind to me, or not caring about me the way I knew I deserved, he will not be dismissive of it. He will not defend them, while I desperately needed him to be by my side. He will not be be so consumed with people pleasing in his friendships that he violates the trust of his closest friend that shared a bed with him every night.
When you have that moment, wherever you may be, I hope the person lying next to you never feel the desolation that once was mine.
My pain was enough for both of us.

And then there were two

You and I have gone through heartbreak together
more than once.
First your brothers, then your father.
I've watched you lay at the front of the door hoping he'd
return while simultaneously lay at the feet of my bed
when depression paralyzed me.
I'm so sorry I wasn't strong enough to console you.
I hated that you had to see me like that.
I hated that all I could do at times is just feed you and go
back in the bed.
I know you heard the nightmares I struggled with.
I know you heard all the muffled tears in the middle of
the night.
I know you got tired of seeing the house so messy.
I know at times you would have preferred to go sit on your
favorite chair.
But you wouldn't leave the room with me in the bed,
You wouldn't leave the room when I was shattered.
And they say cats are cold and aloof.

Closure

You keep chasing closure.
The violation of your boundaries,
Letting you know weren't a priority.
Never having your back the way you had theirs,
Never really giving your props,
comfortably allowing people to speak poorly about you,
Being dismissive of your pain...
That wasn't enough closure for you, love?

Your standards are too high

Standards only scare off people who aren't meant for you.

Wrong Location

Stop expecting to be loved by someone that you can clearly see don't love themselves.

Confidence Vampires

At some point, you have got to stop attracting people in your life that make you feel like you're asking for too much. They're eating away at your confidence.

It's Personal

They'll watch your stuff but secretly act like they don't see it,
They watch strangers support, but barely acknowledge your accomplishments.
They're haters.
Yes, it's personal.
No, it's not your problem.
Bloom louder.

Real Talk

The friendship ended because you were jealous and I got tired of pretending that I didn't see it.

Careful

Just because I've given you grace for not showing up for me the way I needed you to
doesn't mean you can't exhaust my patience.

Just so you know

I will always hold you accountable.
Because the consequence of not doing so will be resentment.

The sharpest knife

Having a friend hate on you is a different form of betrayal.

Silence

If your friends are silent when you're winning,
they are not your friends.

Playing Small

Never shrink your accomplishments to make others comfortable with what they settled for.

Advice

People will project their opinions from their wounds.
Use wisdom and discernment when asking for the opinion of others.
Especially those closest to you.

Your Strong friend

It's not about checking on your "strong friend"
It's about checking your perception about that friend.

Fraudulent

The real ones can always see through performative vulnerability.

Scenes from an immigrant's life

This was a new territory for you.
You were alone
With a young child, in a new country
You carried unhealed trauma from one land to another.
no support,
No capital,
Your degree, worthless.
How alone you must have felt.
I know the responsibility was overwhelming.
I know the isolation was crushing,
I know you didn't have the language for your depression.
And I know the neglect wasn't intentional.
But I was a child.
I didn't know how to help you.
If I did, I would have covered you.
I would have tried to make it less lonely for you.

How disappointing

The problem is we learned how to fight
But we never learned how to reconcile.
We had so much more to offer to each other.

Meditation Pause

Take a deep breath in like you're
smelling your favorite flower,
now blow it out like you're blowing out a candle.

Part IV: Growth and Transformation

Inner child vs Inner Teens

Your inner teen remembers everything in spaces where your inner child has suppressed them.

Inner teen healing

Victimization is a friend of your inner teen. It validates their anger.

You're Responsible

Your anger is valid even when it's dismissed,
But it is still your responsibility to learn the tools to manage it.

Hopelessness

It's easy to choose temporary comfort when you feel like you have nothing else to give.

Trauma Response

Where there is neglect,
You'll find someone living in survival mode.

Triggers

Those of us who've lived in survival mode most of our lives
can recognize the triggers clearly.
Financial unknown,
Inconsistency,
discrimination.
They always create a fight or flight response.
Be kind to yourself,
this is the only version of life you know,
The good news is that it's not the only one that exists.

You never got to meet her

Loving you on survival mode never allowed you to see me in my glory.
I would have loved to love you as this version of myself.

To the strong black woman

It's okay if you're still struggling with stillness.
your ancestors were conditioned to always hurry and rush.
They were beaten, punished, and starved when they were too slow.

Your generation is facing the trauma of being still.
Be kind to yourself as you unlearn hustle and discover what rest looks like on your body.
It's okay if you're still struggling with fragility and gentleness.
You were conditioned to wear your strength as a badge of honor.

Your pain and anger were so easily dismissed that your depression showed up as rage.
What a privilege it must be to choose a "soft life" without the linger of generational trauma. You shouldn't expect cultural competency from those who don't consider your pain as valid.
It's okay to dedicate a time to cry.

Sometimes the sorrow that the body carries can only be released through tears.
It's okay if you've been crying for a while.

What you can control

There are many things in life we can't control
Participating in our own suffering isn't one of them.

Patterns

Language reveals your thought patterns.

To be clear

> Trauma explains behavior
> It does not excuse it.

Genuine love

The discomfort of hard conversations
is a solid ground for genuine love to bloom.

Scenes from an immigrant's life (part 2)

In general, there are 4 forms of neglect.
Physical
Educational
Emotional
and Medical
You checked all those boxes.
Did you know that neglect is a form of child abuse?
I would have never chosen to raise myself.
The more you reject my truth,
The less compassion I have for you.
You are the only person in my life that I'm still on survival mode with.

Speak

Part of your power is your voice.
Use it even if it's shaking.

Leaving poverty

> I know struggle too well.
> This next chapter belongs to ease.

Mediocrity

Stop marinating in mediocrity.
You have so much in you.
your life life is a reflection of what you believe,
Not what you see,
What you believe.

Behind in life

You feel like you're behind in life because you keep setting dates
and deadlines for goals that requires growth and opportunity love.

Listen

Allowing someone to tell you who they are verses you building a perception of who they are and should be, is the quickest way to help them feel seen properly.
And when they feel seen, they feel genuinely loved by you.

Fake healed

Don't mistake rushing to get over someone
as a form of healing.
You can't rush your healing and it isn't linear.

Sit in it

If you sit in the loneliness long enough,
you realize it was the ego that didn't heal.
Not the heart.

Loneliness

If you don't properly identify loneliness when it shows up, the choices you make during those times will become habits that eventually turn into defaults.

Hard truth

It's hope that asks for a sign,
Not faith.

How to wait

Waiting season is development season
Wait patiently, and confidently.

The thing is

Hard work is a given when it comes to pursuing your dreams.
Wisdom and alignment you must pray for.

Favoritism

Everyone that assume it's favoritism doesn't
understand God's Favor.
Don't try to explain it.
His favor is one of the ways he reveals his glory.
May his glory be all over you.

Happiness

Sometimes your idea of happiness is not something others will ever understand.
That shouldn't prevent you from pursuing it.

The truth about Faith

The same faith that you start with is not the same faith
that's going to carry you through.
Your starter faith did it's part. For this next level,
you need a different dose.
Update and upgrade.

In the midst of it

> Gratitude is a spiritual currency.
> In the midst of chaos,
> make sure you give praise.

Prayer is

Prayer is when you talk to God.
Meditation is when God speaks.

Access Denied

You must learn to deny shame entrance when it tries to creep in your life
due to someone else's mistreatment of you.

Courage

Have the courage to wait in loneliness.
Have the courage to walk away from lack.
Have the courage to forgive those who never took accountability of the pain they caused you.
Have the courage to forgive those who weren't there for you during your hard times.
Have the courage to remove anyone you have a question mark about in your life.
Have the courage to forgive yourself.
Have the courage to begin again, and again, and again.
Courage comes before confidence.

Waiting on the right time.

A new year shouldn't dictate when you choose yourself.
Your life doesn't change by a date. It changes by a decision.

Doubt

Do not negotiate with doubt.

A powerful prayer

One of the most powerful prayers you'll learn to pray during the waiting season is not for patience but rather endurance.

Prosperity

For some of us success looks like
being able to put our rent on automatic.

Prosperity (part 2)

For some of us success looks like being in the presence of those we know would never abandon us.

The 7 C's of Success

Success requires the 7 C's
Courage
Confidence
Compassion
Creativity
Commitment
Community
Communication
That's in love and career.

He kept a tab.

Every tear,
Every sleepless night,
Every rejection,
Every time you got up to try again,
Every time you didn't hold it again those closest to you that didn't support you,
Every time you sent multiple follow-up emails,
Applied for one more grant or program,
Showed up online even though it was completely out of your comfort zone,
Showed up in spaces that other people didn't think you deserved to enter
God saw it.
He kept the tab.
Your success is inevitable.

Doing it alone

Choosing to do it alone in order to satisfy your validation appetite
has stolen more from you than you realize.
Validation and pride are siblings.
They work together to keep you from your purpose.

Habitual

Some of us have spared so many people by keeping quiet
about habits
that they deem as mistakes.

Blinded by Image

If the person that you love caused you pain but is more concerned about their reputation, and image than humbly apologizing to you, they are selfish and they're letting you know that how others view them is more important than how they treat you.

What I know for sure

Whatever someone takes from you, God already has someone ahead to pour it back in you.
Stillness nurtures discovery.

Stillness nurtures discovery

Having genuine friendships that support and celebrate you help heal abandonment issues.

Some people are temporary in your life not because fate slates it that way but because pride did.

Every hard time has an expiration date.

When a woman consistently feel unsafe in her relationship
Insecurity creeps in and it inevitably affects
the sexual health of the relationship.

> Sometimes your boundaries trigger people pleasers. Have them anyway.

Anything we put after I AM we slowly become. The more we practice it, the more it sinks into the subconscious mind, because repetition is the language it knows.

> Discipline will get you farther than motivation.
> Self-sabotage is a form of self-betrayal.

Self-control will save you from a lot of unnecessary pain
And drama.

> Soulmates come in many forms.
> For some, it's a family member.

Prioritize your peace. Wait on purpose not fear.

Meditation Pause

Take a deep breath in like you're
smelling your favorite flower,
now blow it out like you're blowing out a candle.

Epilogue

Thank you for taking the time to read my book. I have a goal of having 100,000 people read this book. You can help make it happen if you pass it down, write some reviews, and recommend it to your friends and family. I believe that there's something for everyone that picks up this book. These thoughts need a new home - let's get them there because they can no longer live with me.

Thank you for supporting me on this journey. Keep up with me:

Website: www.HernameisYoumie.com
Instagram: @hernameisyoumie

www.ingramcontent.com/pod-product-compliance
Lightning Source LLC
Chambersburg PA
CBHW020336010526
44119CB00001B/1